11/03

THE *Delaware* COLONY

SPIRIT
of America®

THE *Delaware* COLONY

By Jean F. Blashfield

Content Adviser: Eric Gilg, Department of History, University of
Massachusetts, Amherst, Massachusetts

The Child's World®
Chanhassen, Minnesota

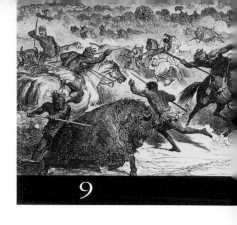

THE *Delaware* COLONY

Published in the United States of America by The Child's World®
PO Box 326 • Chanhassen, MN 55317-0326 • 800-599-READ • www.childsworld.com

Acknowledgments
The Child's World®: Mary Berendes, Publishing Director

Editorial Directions, Inc.: E. Russell Primm, Editorial Director; Melissa McDaniel, Line Editor; Elizabeth K. Martin, Assistant Editor; Olivia Nellums, Editorial Assistant; Susan Hindman, Copy Editor; Joanne Mattern, Proofreader; Kevin Cunningham, Peter Garnham, Ruthanne Swiatkowski, Fact Checkers; Tim Griffin/IndexServ, Indexer; Cian Loughlin O'Day, Photo Researcher; Linda S. Koutris, Photo Selector

Photo
Cover: North Wind Picture Archives; Bettmann/Corbis: 7, 11, 13, 14, 15, 16, 23-top, 23-bottom, 24, 32; Bridgeman Art Library: 17, 30; Corbis: 9 (Chris Hellier), 19, 27 (Kevin Fleming), 33 (Dennis Degnan), 34 (Joseph Sohm; Visions of America); Getty Images/Hulton Archive: 6, 10, 12, 20, 25, 28, 31; North Wind Picture Archives: 21, 22; Stock Montage: 18, 29.

Registration
The Child's World®, Spirit of America®, and their associated logos are the sole property and registered trademarks of The Child's World®.

Library of Congress Cataloging-in-Publication Data
Blashfield, Jean F.
  The Delaware Colony / By Jean F. Blashfield.
      p. cm. — (Our colonies)
  "Spirit of America."
  Summary: Relates the history of the Colony of Delaware from its founding by David Pietersen de Vries in 1631 to its statehood in 1787. Includes bibliographical references (p.) and index.
    ISBN 1-56766-610-8 (alk. paper)
   1. Delaware—History—Colonial period, ca. 1600–1775—Juvenile literature. 2. Delaware—History—1775–1865—Juvenile literature. [1. Delaware—History—Colonial period, ca. 1600–1775. 2. Delaware—History—1775–1865.] I. Title. II. Series.
  F167.B63 2003
  975.1'02—dc21   2003003767

16   25   33

Contents

Chapter ONE

The Original People

The Lenni-Lenape lived in the area now known as Delaware for many centuries before the arrival of Europeans.

THE NATIVE AMERICANS LIVING IN THE AREA now known as Delaware called themselves the Lenni-Lenape, or just Lenape. In their language, Lenape means "true men" or "original people."

The longer name, Lenni-Lenape, means "people who are the standard." They lived in the north. Another Native American group, the Nanticoke people, lived in the southern part of what is now Delaware. All Lenni-Lenape people belonged to one of three large family groups called clans. The three clans were the Turtle, Wolf, and Turkey. Most people in Delaware were in the Turtle clan.

The Lenape did not live as a single community. They lived in separate villages along rivers or streams. They did not have one council or chief who led them all. Instead, each band or village governed itself.

The Native Americans of Delaware probably first encountered the white faces of Europeans in 1524 when they saw the Italian explorer Giovanni da Verrazano. The French had hired him to explore the east coast of North America.

The first Europeans to arrive in the area called the Native Americans there the Delaware, after the bay and the river flowing into that bay. The first hundred years of being around white people brought devastation to the Lenni-Lenape. They were killed by terrible diseases such as smallpox, which the white men

When he arrived in 1524, Giovanni da Verrazano was probably the first European ever seen by Native Americans in Delaware.

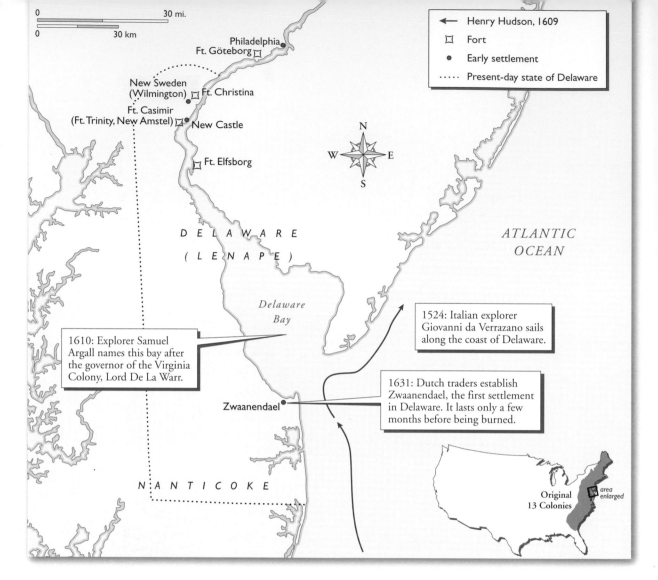

Map labels:

0 — 30 mi.
0 — 30 km

Legend:
← Henry Hudson, 1609
⌂ Fort
• Early settlement
⋯ Present-day state of Delaware

Philadelphia
Ft. Göteborg

New Sweden
(Wilmington) — Ft. Christina

Ft. Casimir
(Ft. Trinity, New Amstel) — New Castle

Ft. Elfsborg

N
W — E
S

DELAWARE
(LENAPE)

ATLANTIC
OCEAN

Delaware
Bay

1524: Italian explorer
Giovanni da Verrazano sails
along the coast of Delaware.

1610: Explorer Samuel
Argall names this bay after
the governor of the Virginia
Colony, Lord De La Warr.

1631: Dutch traders establish
Zwaanendael, the first settlement
in Delaware. It lasts only a few
months before being burned.

Zwaanendael

NANTICOKE

Original
13 Colonies

area
enlarged

Delaware Colony at the time of the first European settlement

had brought from Europe. The Native Americans had never before been exposed to these diseases, so their bodies could not fight them. Their numbers dropped from about 20,000 to 4,000.

In the early 1700s, the Lenni-Lenape were forced into western Pennsylvania. Later, they were pushed into Ohio. There, the different bands united as one group. In time, they ended up in Oklahoma and Ontario, Canada.

8

NATIVE AMERICAN FAMILIES IN THE DELAWARE REGION LIVED IN WIGWAMS. These were round, dome-shaped huts covered in bark. People dressed in clothing made of animal skins. Often, their clothing was decorated with beads, copper strips, and dyed porcupine quills. The women painted themselves a reddish color with a clay called ocher. Men had tattoos.

In summer, several hundred people lived in Lenni-Lenape villages. The women farmed, growing tobacco, corn, squash, beans, and sweet potatoes. The men hunted and fished. They often traveled by **dugout** canoe. During the winter, families spread out to hunt. After Europeans arrived in the region, hunting became even more important to the Lenni-Lenape, because the Native American hunters could exchange furs for goods they needed.

Chapter TWO

The Europeans Arrive

Delaware was named for Thomas West, Lord De La Warr, governor of the Virginia colony.

IN 1609, ENGLISH EXPLORER HENRY HUDSON sailed to North America. The Dutch East India Company had paid for his voyage. He was to search for a water route to the Pacific Ocean. Hudson saw, but did not explore, the land that would later be named Delaware. In 1610, another English explorer, Samuel Argall, named the bay after the governor of the Virginia Colony, Thomas West, Lord De La Warr.

Because of Hudson's voyage into Delaware Bay, the Dutch claimed the right to settle Delaware. Dutch traders sent the first European settlers to Delaware in 1631. Twenty-

eight brave people, led by Captain David Pietersen de Vries, built a settlement on Lewes Creek. They called it Zwaanendael, which means "valley of swans." When a Dutch settler got into an argument with a Native American leader and killed him, a group of Lenni-Lenape killed the colonists and burned down the settlement.

In 1638, Swedish colonists began a new settlement called New Sweden, located where Wilmington is today. The settlers built a fort, which they called Fort Christina after the 12-year-old queen of Sweden. The river that flows through Wilmington is still called the Christina River.

New Sweden grew as both Swedes and Finns brought their families to the new land. They arrived on ships loaded with more supplies. The

Swedish settlers arrived in Delaware in 1638. They started a settlement called New Sweden where the city of Wilmington is today.

▶ When the Lenni-Lenape were forced to move into western Pennsylvania, they dug up the bodies of their chiefs and took them along.

Sandhocken, war ock en Skantz som de Hålländske hafwa låtit bygga uppå de Swenskas Land/ emot Gou-

Gouverneurns åtskillige protester, den de kallade Fort Casimir; Hwarföre ock the Swenska månde den 1654. med storm intaga och Holländerne således der ifrån igen utdrifwa: då han sedan efter Ing. P. Lindströms Ritning och afmätning så godt som af grund å nyo mycket fastare tillika med utan wärcken wart fortificerat och förbättrat/ och sedan H: Trefaldighets FORT kallat.

Manataanung, Manaates, är ock en Platz som Holländerne bebodde/ der på hafwa the bygdt en wacker liten Stad/ hwilken tog mer och mer augment hwar dag/ och blef en skiön kiöpstad utaf/ at der wankades allehanda Saker fahla/ lika som uti sielfwa gamla Holland/ tjt och the Swenska åhrligen hade sin seglas ifrån Nya Swerige/ til at kiöpslaga hwad the hade behof/ och ligger 100. Tyska mjl ifrån wåra i Sidwägen. Der woro också då någre Platzar/ som the Americaner hade sine besynnerlige Planterings och Bonings tilhåld uppå/ hwilka efter theras Nation sålunda namngåfwes.

Mechakanzijåå, ther hade de sina wissa Plantas och hemwist/ tjt ock the Swenska så wäl som de andra Cronans Nationer der ute/ alltjd reste Sidwägen/ til at kiöpa Magiis eller deras egenteliga Lands-Säd/ och ligger 16. Tyska mjl öster ifrån wåra.

Santhickan, der är et Strömfall/ hwarest the ock hade et Plantas på en wjd slät Platz.

Arakunsickan, Thomehettikon och Pimypacka äre ock deras Plantas Land/ af hwilka det senare är mycket fett och fruchtbårande.

Tennako Manaatet, är et Öland och jämwäl af dem beplantades. Utaf desse Plantas-Landen hafwa de ock sina

The Dutch built Fort Casimir where New Castle, Delaware, is located today.

colonists built farms, homes, businesses, and churches. The ships returned to Sweden with furs and tobacco. New Sweden always remained a rather small settlement, however.

In the 1640s, the Swedes built more settlements along the Delaware River. But the Dutch, who had a colony farther north called New Netherland, were also building settlements in that region. They built Fort Casimir where New Castle is today. From this fort, Dutch soldiers controlled all ships heading up the Delaware River.

12

In 1654, New Sweden's governor, Johan Rising, decided to get rid of the Dutch in New Netherland. His troops seized Fort Casimir. But the following summer, Dutch governor Peter Stuyvesant sent ships and soldiers to Fort Casimir. The 600 soldiers had no trouble persuading the Swedish settlers, who were greatly outnumbered, to give up. The Dutch

A cargo of slaves arrives in the colonies on a Dutch ship. The Dutch, who introduced slavery to the English colonies in North America, allowed slavery in Delaware.

New Amsterdam was the center of the Dutch colony of New Netherland, which included the present-day states of New York, New Jersey, Pennsylvania, and Delaware.

leader allowed the Swedes and Finns to form their own government and to keep their land. The Dutch also took over Fort Christina.

By this time, several hundred people lived in the area around Fort Casimir. Some of them were enslaved workers. The Swedes in Delaware did not allow slavery, but the Dutch did. The Dutch began to kidnap Africans and brought them to America as enslaved workers.

Meanwhile, the English were taking over most of the East Coast. By the 1660s, they controlled almost everything from Maine to the southern border of Carolina. But they still didn't control the central part. This was the

As governor, Peter Stuyvesant worked to improve housing and started a market and a yearly cattle fair.

Dutch colony of New Netherland, which included what are now New York, New Jersey, Pennsylvania, and Delaware.

King Charles II of England told his brother James, the Duke of York, that he could have New Netherland if he could take it from the Dutch. James sailed a fleet of ships to Manhattan and pointed the ships' guns at the fort protecting Governor Peter Stuyvesant's home. Not surprisingly, the Dutch settlers gave up.

15

▸ The Duke of York's 18-year rule of Delaware was firm. When Delaware colonist Marcus Jacobsen objected publicly to the Duke's government, he was shipped off to a Caribbean island to work as a slave.

On September 8, 1664, New Netherland became an English colony called New York. Delaware was part of it.

When Peter Stuyvesant surrendered to the English in 1664, all of New Netherland, including Delaware, became the English colony of New York.

THE DUTCH COLONY IN NORTH America did not last long. But Dutch traditions left an important mark on American culture. The Dutch had chosen Saint Nicholas as the **patron saint** of New Amsterdam (present-day New York City). It was a Dutch tradition to have children leave their shoes out to receive gifts on December 6, Saint Nicholas's birthday. Gradually, the name of the gift-giving Saint Nicholas evolved into Santa Claus, and the gift-giving date was moved to Christmas Eve.

The Dutch also brought ice skating to North America. Back in the Netherlands, the Dutch often skated on canals. In those areas of New Netherland where rivers and lakes froze in winter, skating quickly became a popular sport.

Chapter THREE

The Lower Counties

Admiral William Penn (above) died without ever seeing North America. But Pennsylvania was named after him.

THE PART OF THE NEW YORK colony that would become Pennsylvania and Delaware did not grow as fast as the part that would become New York and New Jersey. King Charles II had owed a sum of money to a British Admiral, William Penn. When Penn died in 1671, his son, also named William, inherited the claim to that debt. In 1681, the king finally paid off what he owed. But instead of money, he gave the younger Penn the slower-growing part of New York colony. The king called this new colony Pennsylvania (meaning "Penn's woods"), after Admiral Penn.

The younger William Penn belonged to the Religious Society of Friends, whose members are called **Quakers.** Quakers believe that everyone is equal in the eyes of God. This belief angered the English leaders. Quakers also do not believe in war. This caused them trouble when the English army needed soldiers. Quakers, including Penn himself, were **persecuted** in England. Penn wanted his new colony to be a place where Quakers and others could practice their religions freely, without being mistreated.

Penn realized that the one problem with Pennsylvania was that it did not have an outlet to the sea. He asked the king to add a southern

William Penn receives the charter for Pennsylvania from King Charles II. At the time, Delaware was part of Pennsylvania.

Although William Penn made a treaty with Tammamend, the Lenni-Lenape were forced out of Delaware. This was because Penn's sons dealt unfairly with the later chief, Tishcohan (above).

section along the Delaware River to his colony. The king agreed. The Lower Counties—which is what Delaware was first called— became part of Pennsylvania.

Penn arrived in Pennsylvania with about 100 colonists in late 1682. He believed that people had the right to govern themselves. Penn planned a government in which the people of each county would be represented in both a council and an **assembly.** The representatives would be elected by white male landowners. The council had the power to suggest laws. The assembly would approve the laws. Women, blacks, and white men who did not own land were not represented in Penn's government. Later, Penn decided that Pennsylvania should have a governor who would be elected by the council and the assembly.

Penn promised that he would never mistreat the Native Americans of Pennsylvania. He worked out a treaty of friendship with Tammamend, the Lenni-Lenape chief. This agreement gave Penn the right to build a settlement that was the start of the city of Philadelphia. (After his death, Penn's sons did not keep his promise. The Lenni-Lenape were later forced out of Delaware.)

At first, the colonists of Delaware felt they were treated well as part of Penn's colony. But as more people moved to Pennsylvania, the people in the Lower Counties were outnumbered. Representatives from Pennsylvania soon dominated the assembly. The colonists in the Lower Counties began to complain.

Penn, who had returned to England, came back to Pennsylvania in 1699. He agreed to let the people of Delaware have a separate government. In November 1704, representatives from the Lower Counties met at New Castle in their own assembly. Because Delaware was not a separate colony, however, the governor of Pennsylvania had the power to approve or deny laws made by Delaware's assembly. He rarely interfered, though.

In the following years, more and more people came to Delaware. Most settlers were farmers. They grew crops such as wheat, corn, and rye.

Some of the farmwork was done by indentured servants and slaves. Indentured servants were Europeans who wanted to move to America but

William Penn allowed the people of Delaware to have their own government. The representatives of this Delaware government met at New Castle.

Most of the settlers in Delaware were farmers.

Interesting Fact

▶ Wilmington, Delaware, became the center of wheat milling in the colonies because of its great water power and growing shipping industry.

could not afford to pay their own way. So they agreed to work for a certain period of time—usually five years—in exchange for the fare to America. When landowners couldn't find enough people who wanted to be indentured servants, they bought slaves. In 1721, there were about 500 enslaved workers in Delaware, mostly in the southern part of the colony.

In northern Delaware, industry grew. Mills were built around the city of Wilmington. These mills turned wheat into flour. Other people in Delaware set up sawmills or were craftspeople. Shipbuilding also became a big business.

Delaware was growing and prospering. But, like all the colonies, Delaware would soon experience great upheaval. Revolution was just around the corner.

OBSERVATIONS

For determining the Length of

A DEGREE OF LATITUDE

In the Provinces of MARYLAND and PENNSYLVANIA, in NORTH AMERICA:

By Messieurs CHARLES MASON AND JEREMIAH DIXON.

To which is prefixed

AN INTRODUCTION:

By the Rev. NEVIL MASKELYNE, B.D.F.R.S. ASTRONOMER ROYAL.

LOOK AT DELAWARE ON A MAP. It has a very unusual northern border—it's round. The king's land grant to William Penn called for the southeastern border of Pennsylvania to be an arc drawn exactly 12 miles (20 km) from New Castle.

In the 1760s, two Englishmen, Charles Mason and Jeremiah Dixon, were hired to determine the exact border between Maryland and Pennsylvania. The border between Maryland and Delaware was decided at the same time. The east-west line they decided on became known as the Mason-Dixon Line. It became the unofficial line between the northern and southern states.

Chapter FOUR

The American Revolution

Competition between the British and French for control of the Ohio River valley led to the French and Indian War.

THROUGHOUT THE 1700S, BRITAIN AND FRANCE had often fought over the rich farmland and fur trade in the Ohio River valley. In 1754, this competition turned into the French and Indian War. Though the fighting took place west of Delaware, the war would greatly influence the future of the colony.

The British finally defeated the French in 1763, gaining control of Canada and all land east of the Mississippi River. But this victory had cost a great deal of money. The British wanted the colonies to pay the cost of fighting that war.

Parliament, the law-making part of the British

government, passed a number of taxes on the colonists. The first was the Stamp Act of 1765. It required that a costly stamp be put on all official papers and newspapers. All across the colonies, people howled in protest. Some Delaware officials refused to use the stamps. A meeting of representatives from different colonies was held in New York City to decide what to do about the Stamp Act. Delaware sent John Dickinson, Caesar Rodney, and Thomas McKean to the meeting. Soon the British ended the Stamp Act.

But right away they passed other taxes on items such as paint, lead, paper, and tea. Again the Americans complained. Since they had no voice in the British government, they had no say in approving those taxes. They called it taxation without representation.

In 1774, representatives from the colonies gathered at another meeting, called the First **Continental Congress. Delegates** from all colonies except Georgia met in Philadelphia from September 5 to October 26. Again, Rodney and McKean represented Delaware, this time along with George Read. The Continental Congress sent a letter to Parliament outlining their

Thomas McKean was one of Delaware's representatives at the First Continental Congress.

The Battle of Lexington, fought on April 19, 1775, was the start of the American Revolution.

complaints. Parliament paid no attention.

Then, on April 19, 1775, British troops tried to capture military supplies in Concord, Massachusetts. Samuel Prescott and Paul Revere rode to warn colonial soldiers that the British were coming. The Americans met the British troops at the nearby town of Lexington. Someone fired "the shot heard 'round the world." The American Revolution had begun.

Soon, the Continental Congress met once again. Delawareans saw no reason to start a real fight. But people from Massachusetts had suffered greatly under the British. They were ready to use guns. Congress created the Continental army and put George Washington of Virginia in charge.

Some delegates to the Continental Congress began to look for ways to achieve independence. The following year, 1776, the Continental Congress asked Thomas Jefferson of Virginia to write out the reasons that the colonies should be independent. This became the Declaration of Independence. The members of the Continental Congress had to vote on the declaration.

The Delaware delegates were divided. Thomas McKean and Caesar Rodney favored breaking away from Britain. George Read was equally certain that the colonies were not ready to break away. Two of the three delegates had to agree for Delaware's vote to count. But Rodney was back home in Delaware. McKean sent an urgent message to Rodney to hurry to Philadelphia to cast his vote. The elderly man rode 80 miles (129 kilometers) during a stormy night to get to Philadelphia on time. The Declaration of Independence was adopted, and even George Read decided to sign it.

Back in Delaware, representatives from the colony's three counties wrote a **constitution** for a new state, separate from both Britain and Pennsylvania. This constitution made it illegal to bring slaves into Delaware to sell. In the coming years, many people in Delaware, especially Quakers, began freeing their slaves. By 1790, Delaware was home to about 9,000 slaves and 4,000 free blacks.

Though the American colonies had declared themselves independent, the people of Delaware knew they still

A statue commemorates Caesar Rodney's famous ride to Philadelphia to sign the Declaration of Independence for Delaware.

Major General Howe commanded the British troops in the only battle of the American Revolutionary War fought in Delaware.

had to fight a war to make it a reality. Nearly 4,000 men from Delaware signed up to serve in the Revolutionary War.

Only one battle was fought in Delaware during the Revolution. The Battle of Cooch's Bridge took place near Newark, Delaware, on September 3, 1777. About 800 soldiers from the Continental army challenged 4,000 of Sir William Howe's troops as they crossed from Maryland into Pennsylvania. The Americans failed to keep the British troops from reaching Philadelphia. Eight days later, the same forces met at the Battle of Brandywine in Pennsylvania. George Washington's troops at Philadelphia also failed to hold the city.

Soon, British troops captured Wilmington, along with Delaware's new governor, John McKinly. The people of Delaware feared that the advancing troops would capture their capital, New Castle. So they quickly moved all their official records to Dover and declared it the new capital. British troops left Wilmington in October 1777. That was the end of the war on Delaware soil.

But the war dragged on elsewhere for years. British and American officials finally signed a peace **treaty** in 1783. The colonies had won their independence.

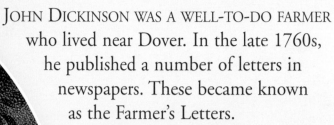

JOHN DICKINSON WAS A WELL-TO-DO FARMER who lived near Dover. In the late 1760s, he published a number of letters in newspapers. These became known as the Farmer's Letters.

The Farmer's Letters protested some of the British taxes. At first, Dickinson did not want America to break with England. But in time, he came to believe that British leaders were stifling freedom in the colonies. Even then, he did not want war. He was a Quaker. He believed in peace, not war.

The arguments Dickinson made in his letters, along with protests by the colonists, convinced Parliament to end most of the taxes. Colonists also agreed with the Delaware farmer on the need for breaking with England. Dickinson became known as one of the founders of American independence.

Chapter FIVE

The New Nation

EVEN BEFORE THE WAR WAS OVER, AMERICANS knew that they had to form a government. The Continental Congress asked Delaware lawyer John Dickinson to write up some laws for the new United States. His idea was to have a strong central government, one with more power than the states had. But most colonists did not want a strong central government. Their experience with the British government had soured them on the idea.

The delegates to the Continental Congress turned down Dickinson's ideas. Instead, they created a **confederation.** They described their new government in a document called the Articles of Confederation.

The Articles of Confederation said more about what the central

Philadelphia's now-famous Carpenters' Hall was the site of the First Continental Congress.

government could not do than what it could do. And it couldn't do very much. The central government was not allowed to pass taxes. There was no money to pay for the new Congress to do anything. Even when the Continental army won

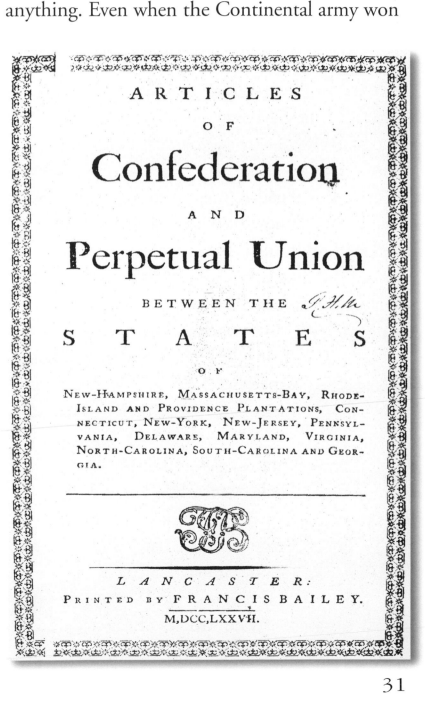

ARTICLES

OF

Confederation

AND

Perpetual Union

BETWEEN THE

STATES

OF

NEW-HAMPSHIRE, MASSACHUSETTS-BAY, RHODE-ISLAND AND PROVIDENCE PLANTATIONS, CONNECTICUT, NEW-YORK, NEW-JERSEY, PENNSYLVANIA, DELAWARE, MARYLAND, VIRGINIA, NORTH-CAROLINA, SOUTH-CAROLINA AND GEORGIA.

LANCASTER:

PRINTED BY FRANCIS BAILEY.

M,DCC,LXXVII.

The Articles of Confederation were the first set of laws governing the United States of America.

31

independence on the battlefield, many soldiers did not get paid.

The Articles of Confederation did not work. Finally, in 1787, the states admitted that something needed to be done. Again, delegates gathered in Philadelphia to discuss problems. They soon realized that the Articles of Confederation could not be fixed. A whole new constitution would have to be written.

John Dickinson was one of Delaware's delegates at the meeting. Dickinson wanted all the states to have equal power in Congress. This was a popular idea among people from small states like Delaware. Other people wanted the number of representatives from each state to be based on that state's population. This would give large states more power.

George Washington addresses the Constitutional Convention in 1787.

In the end, the "Great Compromise" was reached, and the U.S. Congress was created. The Great Compromise gave both large and small states what they wanted. In the Senate, each state is represented equally, whether it is big or small. In the House of Representatives, the number of members from each state is based on population.

Still, some people worried that the Constitution gave the government too much power. Their concerns were answered by the promise that a list of personal rights would be added to the Constitution. This list, called the Bill of Rights, grants Americans many rights, including freedom of speech and freedom of religion.

Interesting Fact

▶ President Thomas Jefferson called Delaware a diamond because it was small but of great value.

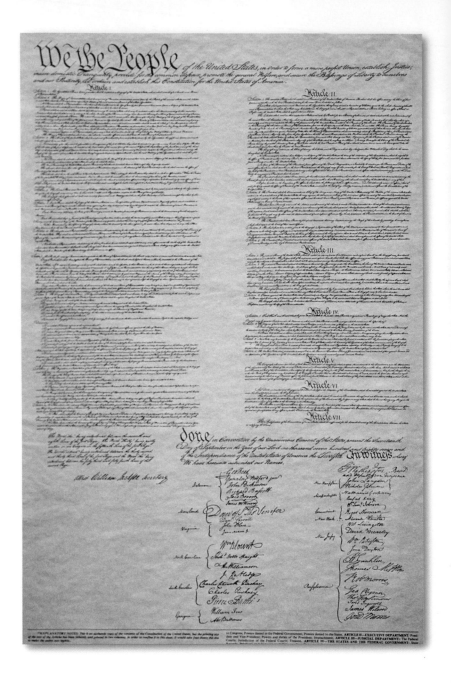

Nine of the 13 states had to approve the U.S. Constitution before it became law. On December 7, 1787, Delaware became the first state to do so. Since then, Delaware has been known as the First State.

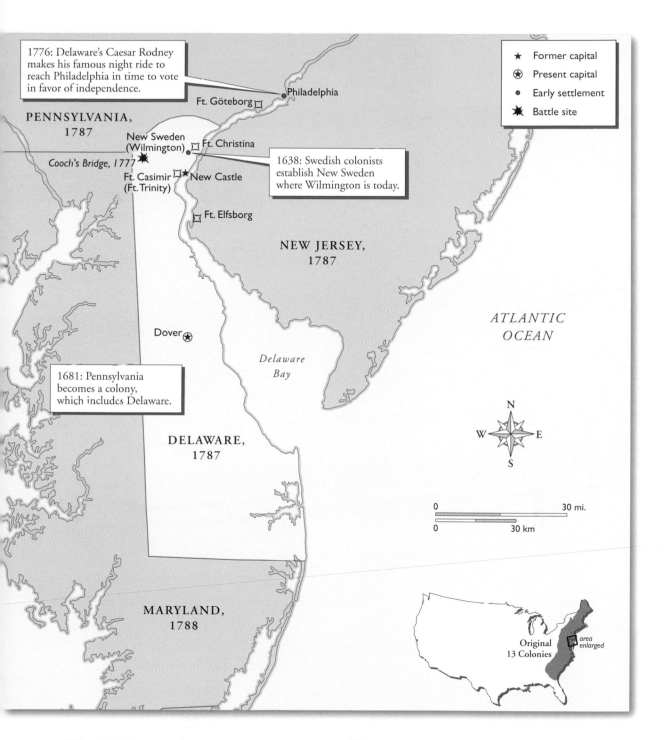

1776: Delaware's Caesar Rodney makes his famous night ride to reach Philadelphia in time to vote in favor of independence.

★ Former capital
⊛ Present capital
● Early settlement
✹ Battle site

Ft. Göteborg ⊡

Philadelphia

PENNSYLVANIA, 1787

New Sweden (Wilmington)
⊡ Ft. Christina

Cooch's Bridge, 1777 ✹

1638: Swedish colonists establish New Sweden where Wilmington is today.

Ft. Casimir (Ft. Trinity) ⊡ ★ New Castle

Ft. Elfsborg ⊡

NEW JERSEY, 1787

Dover ⊛

ATLANTIC OCEAN

Delaware Bay

1681: Pennsylvania becomes a colony, which includes Delaware.

DELAWARE, 1787

N
W   E
S

0 _____ 30 mi.
0 _____ 30 km

MARYLAND, 1788

Original 13 Colonies   area enlarged

The U.S. Constitution went into effect on June 21, 1788, after being approved by the ninth state, New Hampshire. The new nation was born.

Delaware Colony before statehood

1524   Italian explorer Giovanni da Verrazano sails along the coast of Delaware.

1609   Henry Hudson visits the Delaware region, giving the Netherlands a claim to the land.

1610   Samuel Argall names Delaware Bay and Delaware River for Lord De La Warr.

1631   Dutch traders establish Zwaanendael, the first European settlement in Delaware. It lasted only a few months before being burned.

1638   Swedish colonists establish New Sweden, where Wilmington is today.

1654   New Sweden takes Fort Casimir from the Dutch.

1655   The Dutch regain control of Fort Casimir, and New Sweden.

1664   The English defeat the Dutch, turning the Delaware region into part of the British colony of New York.

1681   William Penn receives the land grant to Pennsylvania, which includes what later becomes Delaware.

1704   Colonists in Delaware establish their own government, separate from Pennsylvania's.

1763   Britain defeats France in the French and Indian War.

1765   Britain passes the Stamp Act, the first of many taxes on the colonists. The colonists protest.

1775   The American Revolution begins.

1776   In July, Delaware's Caesar Rodney makes his famous ride to reach Philadelphia, Pennsylvania, in time to vote in favor of independence. Delaware's three counties write a constitution and form the separate state of Delaware in September.

1777   The Battle of Cooch's Bridge, the only Revolutionary battle in Delaware, is fought. Delaware's capital is moved from New Castle to Dover.

1783   The American Revolution ends.

1787   Delaware becomes the first state to approve the U.S. Constitution.

assembly (uh-SEM-blee)
An assembly is a part of government that makes laws. Delawareans complained when they became outnumbered in Pennsylvania's assembly, so William Penn allowed them to form their own government.

confederation (kon-fed-uh-RAY-shun)
A confederation is a group of strong states loosely held together by a central organization. The colonies first attempted to organize as a confederation.

constitution (kon-stuh-TOO-shun)
A constitution is a document outlining the basic laws and structure of a government. Delaware was the first state to approve the U.S. Constitution.

Continental Congress (kon-tuh-NENT-uhl KON-griss)
The Continental Congress was a meeting of colonists that served as the American government during Revolutionary times. The Continental Congress adopted the Declaration of Independence in 1776.

delegates (DEL-uh-guhts)
Delegates are people who represent other people at a meeting. Delaware delegate Caesar Rodney rode all night to get to Philadelphia to vote on the Declaration of Independence.

dugout (DUG-out)
A dugout is a boat made by hollowing out a large log. The dugout canoes of the Lenni-Lenape were crucial to their way of life as hunters and fishers.

patron saint (PAY-truhn SAYNT)
A patron saint is a holy person who some people believe protects a certain place. Saint Nicholas was the patron saint of New Amsterdam (New York City).

persecuted (PER-suh-kyoo-tuhd)
Persecuted people are treated in a cruel or harsh way, often because of their beliefs. Quakers were persecuted in England.

Quakers (KWAY-kuhrs)
The Quakers are a religious group who oppose war and believe that everyone is equal before God. William Penn founded Pennsylvania, which included Delaware, so Quakers would have somewhere to practice their religion freely.

treaty (TREE-tee)
A treaty is an agreement. Americans signed a peace treaty with Great Britain in 1783, officially ending the Revolutionary War.

Delaware Colony's FOUNDING FATHERS

Gunning Bedford, Jr. (1747–1812)
Continental Congress delegate, 1783–85; Delaware attorney general, 1784–89; Constitutional Convention delegate, 1787; U.S. Constitution signer; U.S senator, 1788; U.S. district court judge, 1789–1812

Richard Bassett (1745–1815)
Constitutional Convention delegate, 1787; U.S. Constitution signer; U.S. senator, 1789–93; court of common pleas chief justice, 1793–1799; Delaware governor, 1799–1801

Jacob Broom (1752–1810)
State legislature member, 1784–86, 1788; Constitutional Convention delegate, 1787; U.S. Constitution signer

John Dickinson (1732–1808)
Continental Congress delegate, 1774–76, 1779, 1780; Articles of Confederation drafter, 1776; Delaware president, 1781; Pennsylvania president, 1782–85; Constitutional Convention delegate, 1787; U.S. Constitution signer

Thomas McKean (1734–1817)
Continental Congress delegate, 1774–83; Delaware acting president, Sept.–Oct. 1777; Declaration of Independence signer; Articles of Confederation signer; Continental Congress president, 1781; U.S. senator, 1781–1783; Constitutional Convention delegate for Pennsylvania, 1787; Pennsylvania chief justice, 1777–97; Pennsylvania governor, 1799–1808

George Read (1733–1798)
Continental Congress delegate, 1774–1777; Declaration of Independence signer; Delaware acting governor, 1777; U.S. court of appeals justice, 1782–86; Constitutional Convention delegate, 1787; U.S. Constitution signer; U.S. senator, 1789–93; Delaware chief justice, 1793–98; instrumental in causing Delaware to be the first state to ratify the Constitution

Caesar Rodney (1728–1784)
Stamp Act Congress delegate, 1765; Continental Congress delegate, 1774–76, 1777, 1778; Declaration of Independence signer, 1776; Delaware president, 1778–82; state assembly member, 1776–84

Nicholas Van Dyke (1738–1789)
Continental Congress delegate, 1777–82; Articles of Confederation signer; Delaware president, 1783–86

For Further INFORMATION

Web Sites

Visit our homepage for lots of links about the Delaware colony:
http://www.childsworld.com/links.html

Note to Parents, Teachers, and Librarians:
We routinely verify our Web links to make sure they're safe,
active sites—so encourage your readers to check them out!

Books

Blashfield, Jean F. *Delaware.* Danbury, Conn.: Children's Press, 2000.

Fradin, Dennis Brindell. *The Delaware Colony.* Chicago: Childrens Press, 1992.

Hakim, Joy. *From Colonies to Country.* New York: Oxford University Press, 2003.

Isaacs, Sally Senzell. *Life in a Colonial Town.* Chicago: Heinemann Library, 2001.

Wilker, Josh. *The Lenape Indians.* New York: Chelsea House, 1994.

Places to Visit or Contact

Delaware Agricultural Museum and Village
*To see what life was really like in early Delaware and to watch demonstrations
of crafts from that time*
866 North DuPont Highway
Dover, DE 19901
302/734-1618

Historical Society of Delaware
To learn all about Delaware's past
505 Market Street
Wilmington, DE 19801
302/655-7161

Index

About the Author

JEAN F. BLASHFIELD IS THE AUTHOR OF MORE THAN 100 BOOKS, most of them for young people. She has traveled widely and has lived in Chicago, London, and Washington, D.C. She now lives in Wisconsin—at least that's where her house is. Her mind and her computer take her all over the world (and sometimes beyond).